Our Best
Recipes in a Snap

No-fuss dishes everyone will love!

To cooks everywhere who want to create easy & delicious meals for their family & friends.

Gooseberry Patch
An imprint of Globe Pequot
246 Goose Lane
Guilford, CT 06437

www.gooseberrypatch.com
1 800 854 6673

Copyright, 2021 Gooseberry Patch
978-1-62093-427-2

....

Do you have a tried & true recipe... tip, craft or memory that you'd like to see featured in a **Gooseberry Patch** cookbook? Visit our website at www.gooseberrypatch.com and follow the easy steps to submit your favorite family recipe.

Or send them to us at:
Gooseberry Patch
PO Box 812
Columbus, OH 43216-0812

Don't forget to include the number of servings your recipe makes, plus your name, address, phone number and email address. If we select your recipe, your name will appear right along with it... and you'll receive a FREE copy of the book!

CONTENTS

Make it Easy...Make it in a Snap!

Good food and tasty recipes don't have to be time consuming! If you plan ahead, use all the resources available to you, prioritize your cooking habits and keep often-used ingredients on hand, you can make a meal in a snap! Here are some tricks and tips that you may want to try:

Planning:

Even if you plan ahead, some days are just busier than others. If you know your schedule for the week, plan the simpler meals for those busiest days or choose a slow-cooker recipe if you plan to be gone all day.

Make grocery shopping a planned event. If you shop in the store, make a list that will provide you ingredients for all your recipes for a week. If you shop online, keep a list of what you shop for often and use curbside pickup to save time.

Extra ground beef is tasty in so many easy recipes...tacos, chili and casseroles, to name a few. Brown 3 or 4 pounds at time, divide it into plastic zipping bags and refrigerate or freeze for future use.

Resources:

Buy precut veggies like broccoli flowerets, green pepper strips and sliced onion from the supermarket's salad bar or precut section of the store. Bags of shredded lettuce and cabbage are timesavers too.

Using deli chicken from the grocery store is a real time-saver when you need flavorful cooked chicken in a recipe.

You may be the one that usually cooks the meals, but enlist the entire family to help get the meal together. Younger children can help tear lettuce for the salad and older kids can measure, chop and stir. Everyone can help set the table and help clean up after the meal.

Prioritize:

When you begin cooking your meal, think about the order of preparation. For example, if dinner includes rice or pasta, put the water on to boil before doing anything else. While it is beginning to boil, chop the veggies or prepare the meat that you need to complete the dish.

Move frozen meat into the fridge to thaw overnight. Then it will be ready when you start to cook.

Keep Your Pantry Stocked:
With a well-stocked pantry, hearty meals are just a few minutes away. Quick-cooking thin spaghetti, ramen noodles and instant rice can become basics for all kinds of dishes.

Canned chicken and tuna are useful for cooking up casseroles, soups, salads, sandwich fillings... the possibilities are endless. Keep plenty on hand.

Stock up on a variety of flavorful salad dressings and zingy condiments. They can give salads and sandwiches extra zip and flavor with little effort.

Canned beans and diced tomatoes are delicious and nutritious in hearty soups and chili...they even come already seasoned! Mushrooms, olives and roasted red peppers are flavorful additions too. Purchase a variety of canned items for your pantry so you'll be ready to cook when dinnertime rolls around.

Cinnamon-Apple Breakfast Bowls, p. 19

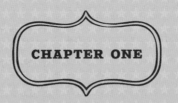

CHAPTER ONE

QUICK-START
Breakfasts

Breakfast Berry Parfait, p. 23

Asparagus & Mushroom Omelet, p. 38

Tiffany Classen, Wichita, KS

Frosty Orange Juice

Thick, frosty and very refreshing! The concentrated orange juice gives it extra flavor.

Makes 4 servings

6-oz. can frozen orange juice
    concentrate, partially thawed
1 c. milk
1 c. water
1 t. vanilla extract
1/3 c. sugar
12 ice cubes

Process all ingredients together in a blender until frothy. Serve in juice glasses.

Jill Ball, Highland, UT

Fruity Cinnamon Oatmeal

There's nothing more perfect than sitting by the fireplace watching the snow fall while eating a warm bowl of oatmeal. This recipe is one of our favorites...it's warm, filling and quick to make.

Makes 4 servings

3 c. water
4-inch cinnamon stick
1-1/2 c. long-cooking oats, uncooked
1 apple, peeled, cored, and diced
3 T. maple syrup, divided
1 t. cinnamon
1/2 t. allspice
Garnish: pomegranate seeds,
    cinnamon

Combine water and cinnamon stick in a small saucepan. Bring to a boil over high heat. Stir in oats and apple; reduce heat to medium. Cook for 5 to 10 minutes, stirring often, to desired consistency. Remove from heat; discard cinnamon stick. Stir in 2 tablespoons syrup and spices. Ladle into bowls; top each with a drizzle of remaining syrup, some pomegranate seeds and a sprinkle of cinnamon.

Fruity Cinnamon Oatmeal

Eleanor Dionne, Beverly, MA

Blueberry Cornmeal Pancakes

Since we like cornmeal muffins as well as anything with blueberries, it's no surprise that these pancakes became a family favorite.

Makes about 24

1 c. all-purpose flour
1 c. cornmeal
2 T. baking powder
1 T. sugar
1-1/2 c. orange juice
3 T. canola oil
1 egg, beaten
1 c. blueberries, thawed if frozen
Garnish: additional blueberries,
    light maple syrup

In a bowl, mix together flour, cornmeal, baking powder and sugar. Add juice, oil and egg; stir well. Gently fold in blueberries. Heat a lightly greased griddle over medium-high heat. Pour batter onto griddle, making small pancakes. Cook pancakes until bubbles appear around the edges; flip and cook on other side. Garnish as desired.

Crystal Shook, Catawba, NC

Peanutty Breakfast Wrap

In a hurry every morning? Don't leave home without a healthy breakfast!

Serves 2

8-inch whole-wheat tortilla
1 T. creamy peanut butter
1 T. vanilla yogurt
1 T. honey
1/4 c. granola
1/4 c. blueberries or diced
    strawberries

Spread one side of tortilla with peanut butter and yogurt. Drizzle with honey; sprinkle with granola and fruit. Roll up tightly; slice in half. Serve immediately, or wrap tightly in plastic wrap and refrigerate.

Peanutty Breakfast Wrap

Vickie, Gooseberry Patch

Mocha Coffee

This homemade version of a favorite coffee-stop drink is easy to make yourself and much faster!

Makes 10 servings

6 T. plus 2 t. instant espresso coffee powder
1-1/4 c. powdered non-dairy creamer
1/2 c. plus 2 t. sugar
3 T. plus 1 t. baking cocoa
1 T. vanilla powder

Combine all ingredients, stirring well. Store in an airtight container. For each serving, add 3/4 cup boiling water to 1/4 cup mix; stir well.

Terry Parke, Indianapolis, IN

Chocolate Scones

Chocolate chips make this scone recipe just a little sweeter! Freeze some for a quick breakfast later.

Makes about one dozen

1 c. sour cream or buttermilk
1 t. baking soda
4 c. all-purpose flour
1 c. sugar
2 t. baking powder
1/4 t. cream of tartar
1 t. salt
1 c. butter
1 c. milk chocolate chips
1 egg, beaten
1 T. vanilla extract
Optional: additional sugar

Combine sour cream or buttermilk and baking soda in a small bowl; set aside. In a large bowl, combine flour, sugar, baking powder, cream of tartar and salt. Cut in butter with a pastry blender; stir in chocolate chips. Add egg and vanilla to sour cream mixture; stir into dry ingredients just until moistened. Turn dough out onto a floured surface; roll or pat out dough into a round about 3/4-inch thick. Cut into wedges or cut out circles with a large, round cookie cutter. Place on greased baking sheets; sprinkle with additional sugar, if desired. Bake at 350 degrees for 12 to 15 minutes, or until golden.

Chocolate Scones

Deborah Wells, Broken Arrow, OK

Cheese & Chive Scrambled Eggs

Paired with hot biscuits, this makes a great breakfast for any day of the week!

Serves 2 to 3

6 eggs, beaten
1/4 t. lemon pepper
1 T. fresh chives, chopped
1/8 t. salt
1 T. butter
1/3 c. shredded Colby Jack cheese
1/3 c. cream cheese, softened

In a bowl, combine eggs, pepper, chives and salt; set aside. Melt butter in a skillet over medium-low heat; add egg mixture. Stir to scramble, cooking until set. Remove from heat; stir in cheeses until melted.

Meg Dickinson, Champaign, IL

Black Bean Breakfast Burritos

My husband and I love the idea of eating breakfast for dinner, so I tried this flavor-filled combination.

Makes 6 burritos, serves 6

2 T. olive oil
1/2 c. onion, chopped
1/2 c. green pepper, chopped
3 cloves garlic, minced
16-oz. can black beans, drained and rinsed
10-oz. can diced tomatoes with green chiles
1 t. fajita seasoning mix
6 eggs
1/2 c. green onion, chopped
1 T. Fiesta Dip Mix
6 8-inch flour tortillas, warmed
1/2 c. shredded Cheddar cheese

Heat oil in a Dutch oven over medium heat. Add onion, green pepper and garlic; sauté until tender. Stir in beans, tomatoes and fajita seasoning. Bring to a simmer and let cook about 10 minutes. Meanwhile, in a bowl, whisk together eggs, green onion and one tablespoon Fiesta Dip Mix. Scramble egg mixture in a lightly greased skillet. To serve, top each tortilla with a spoonful of bean mixture, a spoonful of scrambled eggs and a sprinkle of cheese; roll up tortilla.

FIESTA DIP MIX:
2 T. dried parsley
4 t. dried, minced onion
4 t. chili powder
1 T. dried cumin
1 T. dried chives
1 t. salt

Mix all ingredients well; store in a small jar. Makes about 1/2 cup.

Black Bean Breakfast Burritos

Carol Hickman, Kingsport, TN

Hot Chocolate Muffins

What could be better than hot chocolate? Hot chocolate muffins! You'll love them!

Makes 1-1/2 to 2 dozen

1/2 c. butter, softened
1 c. sugar
4 eggs, separated
6 T. hot chocolate mix
1/2 c. boiling water
2/3 c. milk
3 c. all-purpose flour
2 T. baking powder
1 t. salt
2 t. vanilla extract

Blend butter and sugar together in a large bowl; add egg yolks and beat until well mixed. In a separate bowl, dissolve hot chocolate mix in boiling water; add to butter mixture along with milk. Sift together flour, baking powder and salt; add to butter mixture. In a separate bowl, beat egg whites with an electric mixer on high speed until stiff peaks form; fold egg whites and vanilla into mixture. Pour into greased muffin cups, filling 3/4 full. Bake at 375 degrees for 20 to 25 minutes, until centers test done with a toothpick.

Meri Herbert, Cheboygan, MI

Carroty Bran Muffins

These muffins have so much texture and flavor and stay moist. Keep them refrigerated after baking to keep them fresh.

Makes 1-1/4 dozen large muffins

2-1/2 c. all-purpose flour
2-1/2 c. bran cereal
1-1/2 c. sugar
2-1/2 t. baking soda
1 t. salt
2 c. buttermilk
1/3 c. applesauce
2 eggs, beaten
1-1/2 c. carrots, peeled and shredded
1 green apple, cored and chopped
1 c. sweetened dried cranberries
1/2 c. chopped walnuts
1/4 c. ground flax seed

Mix all ingredients together in a large bowl. Cover and refrigerate batter for up to 2 days, or bake right away. Fill 16 large, greased muffin cups 2/3 full. Bake at 375 degrees for 15 to 18 minutes; do not overbake. Muffins will become moister if allowed to stand for awhile.

Carroty Bran Muffins

Micki Stephens, Marion, OH

Rise & Shine Breakfast Pizza

Tasty layers of all your breakfast favorites!

Serves 8 to 10

32-oz. pkg. frozen shredded
   hashbrowns
1-1/2 c. shredded Cheddar cheese,
   divided
7 eggs
1/2 c. milk
salt and pepper to taste
10 to 12 sausage patties, cooked

Prepare hashbrowns according to package directions; spread on an ungreased baking sheet or pizza pan. Top with 1/2 cup cheese; set aside. Whisk together eggs and milk in a microwave-safe bowl; microwave on high 3 minutes, then scramble eggs well with a whisk. Return to microwave and cook 3 more minutes; whisk well to scramble. Layer eggs on top of cheese; add salt and pepper to taste. Top with remaining cheese. Arrange sausage patties on top. Bake at 400 degrees for 10 minutes or until cheese is melted. Cut into wedges.

Jo Ann, Gooseberry Patch

Cinnamon-Apple Breakfast Bowls

This makes a hearty breakfast, but sometimes we have this for a light dinner too.

Makes 4 servings

1/2 c. quinoa, uncooked, rinsed
   and drained
1-1/4 c. almond milk
1/2 t. vanilla extract
1/4 t. cinnamon
1/8 t. nutmeg
1/8 t. salt
Optional: almond milk, maple
   syrup, chopped pecans, shredded
   coconut

Prepare Maple Roasted Apples. Meanwhile, in a saucepan over medium heat, stir together quinoa, almond milk, vanilla, spices and salt. Bring to a boil; reduce heat to low. Simmer for 10 to 15 minutes, until quinoa is cooked through and liquid has been absorbed. Remove from heat; cover and let stand for 5 to 10 minutes. Fluff with a fork. To serve, divide warm quinoa among 4 bowls; top with apple mixture. Garnish as desired.

MAPLE ROASTED APPLES:
1 T. coconut oil, melted
2 T. maple syrup
1/2 t. vanilla extract
1/4 t. cinnamon
1/8 t. nutmeg
2 Gala apples, quartered and cored

In a bowl, whisk together coconut oil and maple syrup; stir in vanilla and spices. Add apples; toss until coated. Arrange apples on a parchment paper-lined rimmed baking sheet. Bake at 375 degrees for 20 to 25 minutes, basting with pan juices once or twice, until golden. Cool slightly.

Cinnamon-Apple Breakfast Bowls

Julie Dossantos, Fort Pierce, FL

Autumn Morning Smoothie

Our family loves to make breakfast smoothies. After baking pie pumpkins, I decided to try making smoothies for Thanksgiving morning. They were a hit! Now we enjoy them all autumn.

Makes 2 servings

1/2 c. fresh pumpkin purée or
    canned pumpkin
3/4 c. papaya, peeled, seeded and
    cubed
2 bananas, sliced
1/2 c. vanilla yogurt
1/4 c. orange juice
4 ice cubes
1-1/2 t. cinnamon
Garnish: additional cinnamon

Add all ingredients except garnish to a blender. Process until smooth; pour into 2 tall glasses or bowls. Top each with a sprinkle of cinnamon.

Dale Duncan, Waterloo, IA

Rise & Shine Sandwiches

My family loves these breakfast sandwiches anytime! They're easy to make and easy to adapt to your own tastes.

Makes 8 servings

2-1/4 c. buttermilk biscuit baking
    mix
1/2 c. water
8 pork sausage breakfast patties
8 eggs, beaten
1 T. butter
salt and pepper to taste
8 slices American cheese

In a bowl, combine biscuit mix with water; stir until just blended. Turn onto a floured surface and knead for one minute. Roll dough out to 1/2-inch thickness. Cut out 8 biscuits with a 3-inch round biscuit cutter. Arrange on an ungreased baking sheet. Bake at 425 degrees for 8 to 10 minutes, until golden. Meanwhile, in a skillet over medium heat, brown and cook sausage patties; drain. In a separate skillet over low heat, scramble eggs in butter to desired doneness; season with salt and pepper. Split biscuits; top each biscuit bottom with a sausage patty, a spoonful of eggs and a cheese slice. Add biscuit tops and serve immediately.

Light & Fluffy Pancakes

Jessica Dekoekkoek, Richmond, VA

Upside-Down Eggs & Potatoes

What a fun breakfast for the entire family...you get eggs, cheese and potatoes all in one pan! Be sure to garnish it with salsa or sour cream.

Serves 6

2 to 3 T. olive oil
1 to 2 potatoes, shredded
1-1/2 t. garlic powder
1-1/2 t. onion powder
1/2 t. paprika
1-1/2 c. shredded Mexican-blend
   cheese
6 eggs
salt and pepper to taste
Garnish: sour cream, salsa

Heat oil in a deep 10" oven-proof skillet over medium heat. Pat potatoes dry and place in a bowl; add seasonings and toss to mix. Add potatoes to skillet. When about half cooked, use the back of a wooden spoon to smooth out potatoes over the bottom and up the sides of the skillet to form a crust with no holes. Add cheese in an even layer. Beat eggs very well; add salt and pepper to taste. Gently pour eggs over cheese.

Bake, uncovered, at 375 degrees for 20 to 25 minutes, until a knife tip inserted in center comes out clean. Carefully unmold onto a serving plate. Let stand 10 minutes before cutting into wedges. Serve with sour cream and salsa.

Cheri Maxwell, Gulf Breeze, FL

Break-of-Day Smoothie

Make this just the way you like it, using your favorite flavors of yogurt and fruit.

Serves 2

15-1/4 oz. can fruit cocktail
8-oz. container vanilla yogurt
1 c. pineapple juice
6 to 8 ice cubes
Optional: 3 to 4 T. wheat germ

Combine all ingredients in a blender. Blend until smooth.

BBQ Chicken Pizza

Jen Stout, Blandon, PA

Fajita & Bowties Salad Bowl

You'll love this spicy salad for a quick cold lunch.

Serves 4

1/4 c. lime juice
1 T. ground cumin
1/2 t. chili powder
1/2 c. fresh cilantro, chopped
1/2 c. olive oil
15-oz. can black beans, drained and rinsed
11-oz. can corn, drained
1 c. salsa
2 tomatoes, chopped
8-oz. pkg. bowtie pasta, cooked
2 c. tortilla chips, crushed
1 c. shredded Cheddar cheese

Combine lime juice, spices and cilantro in a food processor or blender. Process until almost smooth; drizzle in oil and process until blended. Set aside. In a large bowl, combine beans, corn, salsa, tomatoes, pasta and lime juice mixture; toss to combine. Gently mix in tortilla chips and cheese.

Lucy Davis, Colorado Springs, CO

Lucy's Sausage Salad

This deliciously different salad may be made ahead and chilled for one to 2 hours, or served immediately. It is so quick to make!

Serves 4

14-oz. pkg. mini smoked beef sausages, divided
1 t. canola oil
1 c. corn
15-1/2 oz. can black beans, drained and rinsed
1 T. canned jalapeño pepper, seeded and minced
1 c. red pepper, chopped
Garnish: fresh cilantro sprigs

Measure out half the sausages; set aside for a future use. Slice remaining sausages into 3 pieces each. In a skillet, sauté sausages in oil over medium heat until lightly golden; drain. In a large bowl, combine corn, beans, jalapeño and red pepper. Stir in sausage. Toss with Dressing; garnish with cilantro.

DRESSING:
3 T. plain yogurt
3 T. sour cream
1/4 c. picante sauce
1/2 c. fresh cilantro, chopped
salt and pepper to taste

Whisk together all ingredients.

Audrey Lett, Newark, DE

Suzanne's Tomato Melt

I love this as a quick lunch with a cup of coffee...it is so easy to make!

Makes one serving

1/4 c. shredded Cheddar cheese
1 onion bagel or English muffin,
  split
2 tomato slices
1 T. grated Parmesan cheese
several fresh basil leaves

Sprinkle half the Cheddar cheese over each bagel or English muffin half. Top with a tomato slice. Sprinkle half the Parmesan cheese over each tomato. Add fresh basil leaf on top. Broil about 6 inches from heat for 4 to 5 minutes, or until cheese is bubbly.

Jennifer Oglesby, Brookville, IN

Garden-Fresh Pesto Pizza

With this easy pizza, you can really taste what fresh is all about! I came up with this recipe last year when I had a bounty of cherry tomatoes and fresh basil. The premade crust makes it a quick & easy lunch.

Makes 8 servings

1 ready-to-use rectangular pizza
  crust
1/3 c. basil pesto
1/2 c. shredded mozzarella cheese
1-1/2 c. cherry tomatoes, halved
Optional: fresh basil leaves

Place crust on sheet pan, lightly greased with non-stick vegetable spray if directed on package. Spread pesto over pizza crust and top with cheese. Scatter tomatoes over cheese; add a basil leaf to each quarter of the pizza, if desired. Bake at 425 degrees for about 8 to 10 minutes, until crust is crisp and cheese is lightly golden. Cut into wedges or squares.

Cheddar-Chive Bites

Susanne Erickson, Columbus, OH

Chinese Chicken Wings

Move over, hot wings. These Asian-inspired chicken wings are packed with flavor and they're baked. Make extra, because the crowd will love them!

Makes 2 to 3 dozen, serves 12

3 lbs. chicken wings
1/2 c. soy sauce
1 c. pineapple juice
1/3 c. brown sugar, packed
1 t. ground ginger
1 t. garlic salt
1/2 t. pepper
Optional: celery sticks and ranch
  salad dressing

Place wings in a large plastic zipping bag; set aside. Combine soy sauce and next 5 ingredients; pour over wings, turning to coat. Refrigerate overnight, turning several times. Drain wings, discarding marinade; arrange in a single layer on an ungreased 15"x10" jelly-roll pan. Bake at 450 degrees for 25 to 30 minutes, until golden and juices run clear when chicken is pierced with a fork. Serve with celery and ranch dressing, if desired.

Carrie Helke, Schofield, WI

Deluxe Cocktail Sausages

The surprising combination of brown sugar, pecans and cocktail sausages is super yummy!

Makes 2 dozen

1/2 c. butter
3 T. brown sugar, packed
3 T. honey
1/2 c. chopped pecans
8-oz. tube refrigerated crescent
  rolls, separated
24 mini smoked cocktail sausages

Preheat oven to 400 degrees. As oven is warming, melt butter in oven in a 13"x9" glass baking pan. When butter is melted, add brown sugar, honey and pecans; stir to coat bottom of the pan. Slice each crescent roll triangle into thirds. Roll each smaller triangle around one sausage. Place on butter mixture, seam-side down. Bake, uncovered, at 400 degrees for 15 minutes, or until golden.

Deluxe Cocktail Sausages

Easy Salsa Chili, p. 152

Hunter's Pie

Shannon Hildebrandt, Ontario, Canada

Ground Beef & Kale Curry

This is a simple curry-flavored dish that everyone seems to enjoy.

Serves 4

1 lb. ground beef
1/2 c. onion, chopped
3 cloves garlic, minced
28-oz. can diced tomatoes
1 bunch fresh kale, torn and stalks
    removed
1/2 to 1 T. hot Madras curry powder
salt and pepper to taste
Optional: cooked basmati rice or
    couscous

In a large skillet over medium heat, cook beef, onion and garlic until beef is no longer pink. Stir in tomatoes with juice and kale; add desired amount of curry powder. Reduce heat to low. Cover and simmer for about 15 minutes, stirring occasionally. Season with salt and pepper. Serve plain or over cooked basmati rice or couscous.

Sandra Sullivan, Aurora, CO

Beef & Snap Pea Stir-Fry

In a rush? Spice up tonight's dinner with my go-to recipe for healthy in a hurry! Substitute chicken or pork for the beef, if you like.

Makes 4 servings

1 c. brown rice, uncooked
1 lb. beef sirloin steak, thinly sliced
1 T. cornstarch
1/4 t. salt
1/4 t. pepper
2 t. canola oil
3/4 c. water
1 lb. sugar snap peas, trimmed and
    halved
1 red pepper, cut into bite-size pieces
6 green onions, thinly sliced
    diagonally, white and green parts
    divided
1 T. fresh ginger, peeled and grated
1/2 t. red pepper flakes
salt and pepper to taste
2 T. lime juice

Cook rice according to package directions. Fluff with a fork; cover and set aside. Meanwhile, sprinkle beef with cornstarch, salt and pepper; toss to coat. Heat oil in a skillet over medium-high heat. Add half of beef and brown on both sides. Transfer to a plate; repeat with remaining beef. Stir in water, peas, red pepper, white part of onions, ginger and red pepper flakes; season with salt and pepper. Cook until peas turn bright green, one to 2 minutes. Return beef to skillet; cook for another 2 to 3 minutes. Remove from heat. Stir in lime juice and green part of onions. Serve over rice.

Fettuccine with Smoked Salmon

Pat Crandall, Rochester, NY

Rustic Kielbasa Skillet

This is one of my husband's favorite quick-cook meals, so I make it often. A hearty country bread completes the meal.

Serves 3 to 4

12 new redskin potatoes, quartered
1 to 2 onions, quartered
1 green pepper, diced
1 T. olive oil
3/4 c. chicken broth
2 T. soy sauce
1-1/2 lbs. Kielbasa sausage, sliced
    1/2-inch thick

In a large skillet over medium heat, cook potatoes, onions and pepper in oil until potatoes are golden. Add broth and soy sauce; cook until potatoes and vegetables are fork-tender. Toss in Kielbasa and cook until heated through.

Tami Bowman, Marysville, OH

Speedy Skillet Lasagna

This dish is so quick to make...you don't even have to cook the pasta before you assemble it!

Serves 4 to 5

1 lb. ground turkey
1/4 t. garlic powder
1/4 t. Italian seasoning
2 14-oz. cans beef broth with onion
14-1/2 oz. can diced tomatoes
8-oz. pkg. rotini pasta, uncooked and
    divided
1/2 c. shredded mozzarella cheese
Garnish: 1/4 c. grated Parmesan
    cheese

In a skillet over medium heat, brown ground turkey; drain and add seasonings. Stir in broth and tomatoes with juice; heat to boiling. Add 2 cups uncooked rotini; reserve remaining rotini for another recipe. Cover skillet; cook over medium heat for 10 minutes. Uncover and cook another 5 to 10 minutes until rotini is tender. Stir in mozzarella cheese; top each serving with Parmesan cheese.

Salmon Patties

Jo Ann, Gooseberry Patch

Tangy Citrus Chicken

The molasses in this dish gives it a rich brown color and sweet flavor.

Makes 8 servings

8 boneless, skinless chicken breasts
6-oz. can frozen lemonade, thawed
3/4 c. molasses
1 t. dried savory
1/2 t. ground mustard
1/2 t. dried thyme
1 t. lemon juice

Place chicken in a 13"x9" baking pan coated with non-stick vegetable spray. In a medium mixing bowl, combine remaining ingredients;

mix well. Pour half of the mixture over the chicken. Bake, uncovered, at 350 degrees for 20 minutes. Turn chicken; add remaining sauce. Bake an additional 15 to 20 minutes, or until juices run clear.

Vickie, Gooseberry Patch

Creamy Bacon & Herb Succotash

You'll love this deluxe version of an old harvest-time favorite...I do!

Serves 6

1/4 lb. bacon, chopped
1 onion, diced
10-oz. pkg. frozen lima beans
1/2 c. water
salt and pepper to taste
10-oz. pkg. frozen corn
1/2 c. whipping cream
1-1/2 t. fresh thyme, minced
Garnish: 2 t. fresh chives, snipped

Cook bacon until crisp in a Dutch oven over medium-high heat. Remove bacon, reserving about 2 tablespoons drippings in Dutch oven. Add onion; sauté about 5 minutes, or until tender. Add beans, water, salt and pepper; bring to a boil. Reduce heat; cover and simmer 5 minutes. Stir in corn, whipping cream and thyme; return to a simmer. Cook until vegetables are tender, about 5 minutes. Toss with bacon and chives before serving.

Apricot Layer Bars

Lynda Robson, Boston, MA

Gingerbread Babies

Tuck them into a little box and leave them on someone's doorstep...surely you know someone who will give them a good home at Christmas or any time of year!

Makes about 12 dozen

3/4 c. butter, softened
3/4 c. brown sugar, packed
1 egg, beaten
1/2 c. dark molasses
2-2/3 c. all-purpose flour
2 t. ground ginger
1/2 t ground allspice
1/2 t. nutmeg
1/2 t. cinnamon
1/4 t. salt

In a large bowl, blend together butter and brown sugar until fluffy. Add egg and molasses. In a separate bowl, combine remaining ingredients; gradually stir into butter mixture. Turn dough out onto a well-floured surface; roll out to 1/8-inch thickness. Cut dough with a 2-inch gingerbread boy cookie cutter. Place on greased baking sheets. Bake at 350 degrees for 9 to 10 minutes, until firm.

Dianna Oakland, Titusville, FL

Dianna's Best Tiramisu

I have tried many versions of this dessert...this one is by far the best. Everyone always asks for seconds and the recipe!

Serves 16 to 24

1 c. brewed coffee, cooled
1/2 c. plus 1 T. sugar, divided
2 8-oz. pkgs. cream cheese, softened
2 T. almond-flavored liqueur or
  1/2 t. almond extract
12-oz. container frozen whipped
  topping, thawed
16-oz. pound cake, cut into 30 slices
1 T. baking cocoa

Combine coffee and one tablespoon sugar in a medium bowl; set aside. In a bowl, beat cream cheese with an electric mixer at medium speed, until fluffy. Add remaining sugar and almond liqueur or extract. Gently fold in whipped topping and set aside. Layer 10 cake slices on the bottom of an ungreased 13"x9" baking pan. Brush one-third of coffee mixture over cake slices with a pastry brush. Top with one-third of cream cheese mixture. Repeat 2 more times to create 3 layers. Sprinkle cocoa over top and chill until ready to serve.

Chocolate Pinwheels

Lesleigh Robinson, Brownsville, TN

Chocolate Oatmeal Cookies

I've been making these since I was ten years old. They are the simplest cookies I've ever made...you don't even have to bake them!

Makes about 2 dozen

1/3 c. butter, melted
2 c. sugar
1/2 c. milk
1/3 c. baking cocoa
1/2 c. creamy peanut butter
3 c. quick-cooking oats, uncooked

In a saucepan over medium heat, combine butter, sugar, milk and cocoa. Bring to a boil; cook for one minute. Remove from heat; stir in remaining ingredients. Mix well; drop by rounded teaspoonfuls onto wax paper. Let cookies cool completely.

Judy Lange, Imperial, PA

Ginger Ale Baked Apples

A yummy fall dessert or after-the-game snack!

Serves 4

4 baking apples
1/4 c. golden raisins, divided
4 t. brown sugar, packed and divided
1/2 c. ginger ale

Core apples but do not cut through bottoms. Place apples in an ungreased 8"x8" baking pan. Spoon one tablespoon raisins and one teaspoon brown sugar into center of each apple. Pour ginger ale over apples. Bake, uncovered, at 350 degrees, basting occasionally with ginger ale, for 45 minutes, or until apples are tender. Serve warm or cold.

GOOD IDEA
Some apples work better for baking than others. Braeburn, Cortland, Jonathan, Fuji, Granny Smith, Jonagold and Honeycrisp all work well for baking because they stay firm and hold up well during the baking process.

Ginger Ale Baked Apples

Vickie, Gooseberry Patch

Orange-Filled Napoleons

This dessert looks so fancy but it is so easy to make!

Makes 4 servings

8-oz. pkg. frozen puff pastry sheets, thawed
2 c. vanilla ice cream, softened
1 orange, peeled and thinly sliced
Garnish: powdered sugar

Unfold pastry sheets and cut into 8 rectangles. Place on an ungreased baking sheet and bake at 375 degrees for 20 minutes, or until puffed and golden. Let cool. To serve, split pastries lengthwise. Spoon ice cream on one half; top evenly with orange slices and replace pastry top. Dust with powdered sugar.

Jennifer Holt, Fort Worth, TX

German Chocolate Delights

These cookies are quick to make because you use a cake mix as the dry ingredients for the batter. Adding all the other goodies just makes them yummy!

Makes about 4-1/2 dozen

18-1/4 oz. pkg. German chocolate cake mix
1/2 c. oil
2 eggs, beaten
1 single refrigerated chocolate pudding cup
1 c. semi-sweet chocolate chips
1/2 c. long-cooking oats, uncooked
1/2 c. chopped pecans
1 c. sweetened flaked coconut

Combine dry cake mix and remaining ingredients; blend well. Drop dough by rounded teaspoonfuls, 2 inches apart onto ungreased baking sheets. Bake at 350 degrees for 8 to 10 minutes, until set. Cool one minute before removing from baking sheets.

German Chocolate Delights

Vickie, Gooseberry Patch

Mini Mousse Cupcakes

These little chocolate treats are so pretty served on a dessert tray.

Makes 2 dozen

2-1/3 c. milk chocolate chips
6 eggs, beaten
1/4 c. plus 2 T. all-purpose flour
Garnish: whipped cream, chocolate
    shavings

Melt chocolate chips in a double boiler over medium heat and let cool slightly. In a large bowl, beat eggs and flour. Beat in melted chocolate until combined. Fill paper-lined mini muffin cups 2/3 full. Bake at 325 degrees for 7 to 10 minutes, until edges are done and centers shake slightly. Cool in tin on wire rack for 20 minutes. Remove from tin; cool completely. Garnish with whipped cream and chocolate shavings.

Amy Greenlee, Carterville, IL

Honey-Baked Bananas

My mom shared this recipe for luscious honeyed bananas. They are so quick to make and always a hit!

Serves 6

6 bananas, halved lengthwise
2 T. butter, melted
1/4 c. honey
2 T. lemon juice
Garnish: toasted coconut, lemon
    slices

Arrange bananas in an ungreased 13"x9" baking pan. Blend remaining ingredients; brush over bananas. Bake, uncovered, at 350 degrees for about 15 minutes, turning occasionally. Garnish with toasted coconut and lemon slices.

IN A SNAP
Apples, bananas and tomatoes ripen quickly if placed overnight in a brown paper bag.

Desserts

U.S. to Metric Recipe Equivalents

Volume Measurements

1/4 teaspoon . . . . 1 mL

1/2 teaspoon . . . . .2 mL

1 teaspoon . . . . .5 mL

1 tablespoon = 3 teaspoons . . . . 15 mL

2 tablespoons = 1 fluid ounce. . 30 mL

1/4 cup . . . . 60 mL

1/3 cup . . . . .75 mL

1/2 cup = 4 fluid ounces . . . . . .125 mL

1 cup = 8 fluid ounces . . . . 250 mL

2 cups=1 pint=16 fluid ounces 500 mL

4 cups = 1 quart . . . . .1 L

Weights

1 ounce . . . . 30 g

4 ounces. . . . . 120 g

8 ounces. . . . . 225 g

16 ounces = 1 pound . . . . 450 g

Baking Pan Sizes

Square

8x8x2 inches . . . . .2 L = 20x20x5 cm

9x9x2 inches . . . . . . 2.5 L = 23x23x5 cm

Rectangular

13x9x2 inches . . . . . .3.5 L = 33x23x5 cm

Loaf

9x5x3 inches . . . . .2 L = 23x13x7 cm

Round

8x1½ inches . . . . .1.2 L = 20x4 cm

9x1½ inches . . . . .1.5 L = 23x4 cm

Recipe Abbreviations

t. = teaspoon	ltr. = liter
T. = tablespoon	oz. = ounce
c. = cup	lb. = pound
pt. = pint	doz. = dozen
qt. = quart	pkg. = package
gal. = gallon	env. = envelope

Oven Temperatures

300° F .150° C

325° F . . . . .160° C

350° F .180° C

375° F . . . . .190° C

400° F . . . . 200° C

450° F .230° C

Kitchen Measurements

A pinch = 1/8 tablespoon

1 fluid ounce = 2 tablespoons

3 teaspoons = 1 tablespoon

4 fluid ounces = 1/2 cup

2 tablespoons = 1/8 cup

8 fluid ounces = 1 cup

4 tablespoons = 1/4 cup

16 fluid ounces = 1 pint

8 tablespoons = 1/2 cup

32 fluid ounces = 1 quart

16 tablespoons = 1 cup

16 ounces net weight = 1 pound

2 cups = 1 pint

4 cups = 1 quart

4 quarts = 1 gallon